W9-AOX-226

PREDATOR VS. PREY

Crocodile vs. Wildebeest

Mary Meinking

Raintree

Chicago Illinois

www.heinemannraintree.com
Visit our website to find out more information about Heinemann-Raintree books.

To order:
☎ Phone 888-454-2279
🖥 Visit www.heinemannraintree.com to browse our catalog and order online.

© 2011 Heinemann Library
an imprint of Capstone Global Library, LLC
Chicago, Illinois

Edited by Rebecca Rissman, Dan Nunn, and Catherine Veitch
Designed by Joanna Hinton Malivoire
Levelling by Jeanne Clidas
Picture research by Hannah Taylor
Production by Victoria Fitzgerald
Originated by Capstone Global Library
Printed and bound in China by CTPS

14 13 12 11 10
10 9 8 7 6 5 4 3 2 1

Library of Congress Cataloging-in-Publication Data
Meinking, Mary.
 Crocodile vs. wildebeest / Mary Meinking.
  p. cm.—(Predator vs. prey)
 Includes bibliographical references and index.
 ISBN 978-1-4109-3935-7 (hc)
 ISBN 978-1-4109-3944-9 (pb)
1. Nile crocodile—Food—Juvenile literature. 2. Brindled gnu—Defenses—Juvenile literature. 3. Predation (Biology)—Juvenile literature. I. Title.
 QL666.C925M45 2011
 597.98'2153—dc22
2010016918

Acknowledgments
We would like to thank the following for permission to reproduce photographs: ardea.com pp. 27 (© Ferrero- Labat), 28 (© Ferrero- Labat); Corbis pp. 23 (Andy Rouse), 25 (Joe McDonald); FLPA pp. 4 (Ariadne Van Zandbergen), 8 (Malcolm Schuyl), 13 (Ariadne Van Zandbergen), 17 (Minden Pictures/ Suzi Eszterhas), 19 (Minden Pictures/ Suzi Eszterhas), 21 (Minden Pictures/ Suzi Eszterhas), 18 (Minden Pictures/ Suzi Eszterhas); Getty Images p. 10 (Gallo Images/ Federico Veronesi); istockphoto p. 6 (©Catharina van den Dikkenberg); NHPA p. 29 (Martin Harvey); Photolibrary pp. 5 (Peter Arnold Images/ Martin Harvey), 9 (Imagestate/ Jonathan & Angela Scott), 12 (Oxford Scientific/ Roger de la Harpe), 14 (age fotostock/ Anup Shah), 15 (age fotostock/ Thomas Dressler), 16 (John Warburton-Lee Photography/ Nigel Pavitt), 20 (Oxford Scientific/ Mark Deeble & Victoria Stone), 24 (John Warburton-Lee Photography/ Nigel Pavitt), 26 (Oxford Scientific/ Mike Powles); Rex Features p. 22 (Andy Rouse); shutterstock pp. 7 (©EcoPrint), 11 (©EcoPrint).

Cover photographs of a Nile crocodile reproduced with permission of FLPA (Malcolm Schuyl), and a wildebeest reproduced with permission of shutterstock (© EcoPrint).

We would like to thank Michael Bright for his invaluable help in the preparation of this book.

Some words are shown in bold, **like this**. You can find out what they mean by looking in the glossary.

Contents

Teeth Vs. Horns

Jaws crush! Hooves stomp! Two animals battle on the riverbank. On one side of the battle is the crocodile. Its teeth are sharp and it is ready for action!

crocodile

The other animal in the fight is the wildebeest. Both animals are ready for a fight!

wildebeest

The competitors live in Africa. Both have strengths that will help them in this battle.

PREDATOR
Nile crocodile

LENGTH: 20 feet

WEIGHT: 1,500 pounds

STRENGTH: swallows rocks to help it stay underwater

Key
 where Nile crocodiles and blue wildebeest live

PREY
blue wildebeest

LENGTH: 8 feet

WEIGHT: 507 pounds

STRENGTH: runs very fast on land.

Africa

Toothy Grin

The crocodile is a killing machine! Its eyes, ears, and **nostrils** are on the top of its head. This is handy when it is underwater sneaking up on **prey**.

nostril

Did You KNOW?

Crocodiles can snap their jaws shut harder than any other animal on Earth!

Thundering Hooves

The wildebeest's feet, or **hooves**, are its best protection. If a predator attacks a young wildebeest, the **herd** surrounds the predator. Then they **trample** it with their hard hooves.

hooves

Did You Know?
The name wildebeest came from the local people who call them "wild beasts."

Who's Hungry?

The crocodile is a **carnivore**. It eats other animals. The crocodile can go for almost a month without eating. Wildebeest are **herbivores**. They eat grasses.

Did You Know?
During the dry season the grass in the wildebeest's homeland dries up. So it joins two million other wildebeest looking for fresh grass.

Danger Below

The ground starts to shake! A **herd** of wildebeest has come to cross the river. But first they need a drink of water. The crocodile feels the **vibrations** of the stomping wildebeest. It gets ready for a fight.

A few wildebeest splash into the water. They walk out as far as they can. Then they start swimming toward the other side. Hundreds follow. The crocodile watches the wildebeest crossing the river.

The crocodile looks for a young, old, sick, or hurt wildebeest to attack.

The crocodile spots an old wildebeest. The wildebeest is not looking for **predators**. It is only focused on crossing the river. The crocodile whips its muscular tail from side to side to swim toward the old wildebeest.

Did You Know?

A crocodile will drag its **prey** underwater to drown it before eating it.

The crocodile quietly swims near the wildebeest **herd**. It sinks underwater. In a flash the crocodile chomps down on a wildebeest's leg. The wildebeest stabs at the crocodile with its horns. But its horns are no match for the crocodile's armor-like skin!

The crocodile is not letting go of the wildebeest's leg. It drags the wildebeest toward deeper water and pulls it under. It's trying to drown the wildebeest.

But the wildebeest bobs to the surface and grabs a breath. It struggles to swim. It's not giving up.

Other crocodiles swim to the scene.
They work as a team. Now there is
no way the wildebeest can escape.
While the crocodiles are busy with the
trapped wildebeest, the others quickly
climb out of the river.

And the Winner Is...

...the crocodile! The team of crocodiles rips off huge chunks of flesh. One adult wildebeest provides enough food for several crocodiles.

Did You Know?

Crocodiles' jaws don't move sideways. So they cannot bite off chunks of meat. Instead they bite then spin their bodies to rip off pieces of flesh.

What Are the Odds?

Crocodiles catch their **prey** four out of every five tries! Crocodiles can eat up to half their body weight in food. Sometimes they catch and kill extra food. They store it underwater under a big rock until they are ready to eat it.

Did You Know?
About 200 people are
eaten each year by
Nile crocodiles.

Glossary

carnivore animal that eats meat

herbivore animal that eats plants

herd group of animals living and moving together

hooves hard covered animals' feet

nostril nose opening

predator animal that hunts other animals

prey animal that is hunted by other animals for food

trample walk heavily on something

vibration shaking back and forth motion

Find out more

Books

Encyclopedia of *Animals.* New York: Dorling Kindersley, 2006.

Markle, Sandra. *Crocodiles.* Minneapolis, MN: Lerner Publications, 2004.

Thompson, Gare. *Serengeti Journey: On Safari in Africa.* Washington, DC: National Geographic Society Children's Books, 2006.

Wojahn, Rebecca Hogue and Donald Wojahn. *A Savanna Food Chain: A Who-Eats-What Adventure in Africa.* Minneapolis, MN: Lerner Publications, 2009.

Websites

http://animals.nationalgeographic.com/ animals/mammals/wildebeest.html
This Website is full of facts about wildebeest.

http://kids.nationalgeographic.com/Animals/ CreatureFeature/Nile-crocodile
Find out more about Nile crocodiles, watch a video, and print off collector's cards.

Index

Africa 6

carnivore 12

eating 12, 19, 28, 29

food 26

herbivore 12
herd 10, 14, 20
hooves 4, 10
horns 20

jaws 4, 9, 27

nostril 8

prey 8, 19, 28

river 14, 16, 18, 24
riverbank 4

swim 16, 18, 20, 23, 24

tail 18

underwater 6, 8, 19, 20, 28

water 14, 16, 22